PAGES LEFT
TO TURN

PAGES LEFT TO TURN

Poetry by Restless Minds

Elijah Levy Ph.D.

To order additional copies of this book, contact:
Xlibris LLC
1-888-795-4274
www.Xlibris.com
Orders@Xlibris.com
550778

TABLE OF CONTENTS

Heidi Aichinger 11

Demetrius Franks 23

Steven Maycock 27

Albert Garcia 35

Osvaldo R...39

By Desiree and Osvaldo 43

Desiree Robledo...47

Jay Derifield 57

Boonkiat Rinumpai..61

Eric Williams..65

Marc Spoto and Desiree Robledo.......................................75

Cecile Mermelstein 79

Brenda Kiszonak...95

Barron Odom..99

Pat McCloud 115

Andrew Knight..123

Marc Spoto 173

Christopher Richards 181

Arlene Gardipee..195

ACKNOWLEDGMENT

We couldn't have expressed ourselves without the support, guidance and inspiration of Dr. Elijah Levy who unselfishly helps us cope with our illness so we can strive for a more productive and meaningful life.

Marc Spoto
Demetrius Franks
Paul Alarcon

Acknowledgments by Elijah Levy, Ph.D.

The publication of this anthology owes its inspiration to the remarkable team of mental health professionals at Founders House of Hope. The milieu of unconditional positive regard contributes to sustaining support and hope that the written words could be completed. Unless there's a safe, comforting and reassuring environment, residents would not write and share. The individuals responsible for engendering this therapeutic milieu include Arbie Tolentino, Activity Director; Irma Ruano, Administrator; our Manager Judy Dario and Assistant Manager Francisca Arambulo.

I have been at Founders House of Hope for 18 years, and it represents my true and fitting work. I must express my deep appreciation to Mike and Tess Bolong, and their son Mike Jr. for their enduring support of my work at Founders. I am empowered to implement our recovery program for the residents to achieve their psychiatric rehabilitation goals. I have the resources to enable our residents to reclaim their lives to lead meaningful and self-determined lives.

I want to acknowledge the 25 plus years that Dr. Ted McKnelly dedicated to treating the residents at Founders House of Hope. Ted, you left a significant trace at Founders, one that will never fade and the residents miss you dearly. Your patience and powerful dedication to our residents' recovery and pursuit of meaningful living has been curative and healing in so many ways. I also need to acknowledge Vince and Tess Frias for the years of exceptional care and dedication they provided managing Founders House of Hope. Under their leadership, the program thrived and residents appreciated an enhanced quality of life.

I also want to thank Purandar Mallya, M.D. for volunteering his services at Founders House of Hope. Dr. Mallya understands mental illness and it's debilitating course, and through his gentle, humorous and therapeutic ways, instills hope that a positive, meaningful future is possible for our residents. It's been a wonderful privilege to have Purandar on my team.

DEDICATION

Marc Spoto: To my mom and dad.

Albert: To Pastor George, Sister Ana and Olga Garcia.

Christopher: To all the creative people in the world.

Demetrius: To all the residents at Founders and my loving family.

Pat McCloud: To friends and family, Terri and Larry and especially mom and dad.

Jay: To my father Gerald and my mother Guadalupe.

Ozzy: To my daughter Morama who passed away at two months.

Steve Maycock: To my family.

Barron: To all the people in the world challenged with mental illness.

Brenda: To my family and friends.

Eric: To all my friends at Founders House of Hope.

Desiree: To my mother Shelli, my grandmother Cyndi and my family.

Cecile: To my loving sister Libby.

Heidi: To my family and the residents and staff at Founders House of Hope.

Andrew Knight: To my mom Brenda and my dad John.

HEIDI AICHINGER

Heidi was born in Santa Monica and has lived in California her whole life. She attended Redondo Union High School in Redondo Beach and she played volleyball, basketball and was on the track team. After graduating, she enjoyed art, reading and spending time with her family. Currently, Heidi enjoys writing poetry and writes about life, love and happiness.

TOGETHERNESS

To each his own,
to each of us.

I have happiness.
I have togetherness.
I want to contribute.
I want to share.
I want to laugh.
I want to have fun.
I want to be friendly.
Happiness is what I want.
Happiness is togetherness.

ALONG WITH MYSELF

I want to be myself.
I want to be my own.
I want to be good to myself.
I want to mind my own business.
People have to find themselves.
I want to be loved.
I want to be friendly.
I want people not to fight with each other.

PEACE

Peace is friendship.
Peace is strength.
I want peace of mind.
I want to feel good.
I want to be friendly.
To each hos own.
Friendship is with me.
I want good cheer.
I want to exercise away from harm.

GETTING UP AND GOING

Getting along is fun.
Getting along is peaceful.
Getting along is happiness.
I don't want to argue.
I don't want to fight.
I want to have peace in my heart.

FOREVER

Yesterday was gone.
 Today is here.
I love forever.
I love to be.
I'm happy.
I want to be myself.
I want forever to come.
I want to be me.
Forever and ever I want happiness.

LOVELINESS

Beauty is us.
Beauty is for us.
Beauty is happiness.
I want happiness.
I want to be at peace.
I love people.
I love being myself.

WONDER

Happiness is mine.
Happiness is fine.
Together we are.
Together we go.
I want wonder and peace for my soul.
I want faith and spirit.
Exercising and going is my fun time.

HAPPINESS IS BEING LOVED

Being loved is fine.
Being loved is being reassured.
Being loved is affection.
Being loved is happiness.
Being loved is together.

STRENGTH

Strength is our goal.
Strength is our deed.
Strength is being gratified.
Strength is our human need.
Strength to go forward.
Strength is our comfort.
Strength is our happiness.

OUR PICTURE

O ur picture is our word.
Our picture is our thought.
This is our home and our peace.
Our expression.
Our need.

DEMETRIUS FRANKS

Demetrius began writing while in high school and enjoyed poets such as Maria Rainer Rilke, W.S. Burrows and Samuel Beckett. He attended Poly High School in Long Beach and he excelled in Art and English Literature classes. Demetrius attended Long Beach City College for one year completing general education classes. He enjoys writing prose poetry with irony and is inspired by Rilke's poetry. His writing is about life and relationships. He wrote a novel in 1995 titled Enamel Letter to the Reader, which is about a man searching for purpose in life after his wife left him. Demetrius enjoys watching soccer and spending time with his family who live in Long Beach.

INWARD

The hours pass as weight round the ankles of time.
Ouzo swoons the mind to a meager nirvana.
So, I am numb enough to write.
Inward.
I have sought inward into the self,
I cannot touch, unlocking the doorways
which hold the shackles of the madmen
kept forbidden from my mirror.
I have sought inward discovered and sailed the seven seas of sin.
Seas which harbor nothing but the species of me,
species that will crawl and evolve upon my freak ecology.

STEVEN MAYCOCK

S teven was born in Anaheim, CA and attended La Habra High School. After graduating, he worked as a printer, salesman and other odd jobs. Steven enjoys his private time, likes traveling in Northern California and spending time with his family.

BUMPY

It's been a long bumpy road, fall of obstacles left and right.
Right to left, top to bottom, bottom to top.
Recently I've been stable for a while
and I feel good.
Finally, for the first time in a long time.
It's still a bit of a bumpy ride,
but in a much more structured fashion.

MY GIFT TO YOU

As I take your hand
and as we embrace
only the look of happiness
I will see on your face.
We will always be together.

TOGETHER FOREVER

Together forever, everything changes.
Like seasons in and around the life we live.
If the season didn't change or did change,
there's always something nice and beautiful to give.
We love ourselves.
We like ourselves.
That will always be
something new
always sprouts like the leaves of a tree.

THE MOON, THE SUN, THE BELL

The moon is our light shining so bright.
  So we will never lose our way or always to be a refreshing sight.
The sun sprays its rays over the world well be.
Thank heaven for the moon and the sun as well.
They both guide us, like the toll of a bell.

HARD AND HEAVY

Hard and heavy life sometimes seems.
The more you think it rips and steams.
My way or the highway it doesn't always go.
It seems to me to me to be very happy or sad
is a no show.
Hard and heavy life goes round and round.
Never lost and already been found.

HOPE

To look up.
To look down.
To look forward is the way.
The best ways are all.
Notice everything around yourself.
It's all in open view for you.
And everyone to enjoy.
Watch where you are going is the best way.
Thee maybe bumps in the road.
So watch where you look.
Enjoy life, be content.
If you are not, do some research
on yourself and you'll find
the answer is inside yourself.

ALBERT GARCIA

Albert enjoys working part time and attending groups at Founders. He attended Artesia High School where he liked to write. Albert enjoys spending time in the community, shopping for t-shirts, jackets and backpacks. He also attends Victory Outreach Church in Norwalk where he volunteers at social events. At Founders, Albert has many friends and is popular with the staff.

FINDING GOD

When I gave my life to Jesus Christ,
I didn't realize how good I had it.
I began to read the Bible and realized life could be so good.
At the age of 18, I did my own thing,
and one person asked me to go to Church.
I went to Victory Outreach
and was surrounded by love and compassion.
My spiritual father was Pastor George.

OSVALDO R.

Ozzy was born in Brazil and at the age of one his family moved to Guantanamo Bay, Cuba. He lived in Cuba until the age of 22 before moving to Tucson, Arizona and traveling between Ohio, Cleveland working. At the age of 24 he decided to live in Ohio working as a maintenance worker on a boat. He stayed in Ohio until 1984 when he returned to Tucson. In Tucson he worked in a restaurant as a dishwasher and was promoted to Chef. In 2011, Ozzy moved to Los Angeles and he plans to remain in Southern California. Ozzy has been residing at Founders House of Hope since 2012.

FOUNDERS

I arrived in 2012
and found my home
Where I'm not alone.
I love my work
which is a good hurt.

I'm doing the good work.
Everybody loves me,
so I'll continue to be me.

I attend group,
and learn the scoop.
So I can get in the loop,
which keeps me in the mood.
I want to do the ultimate good.

SO YOU

The sky is blue.
     Sun in my heart
when I'm with you.
I feel so true.
You bring me to you,
and we are two.

BY DESIREE AND OSVALDO

WAITING

The moon and the stars shine so bright.
I am missing you tonight.
The sun shines on the ocean and the seal looks for food.
The moonlight reflects in the midnight waves.
Where have you been?
I've been looking around for so long.
So please come home where you belong.

DESIREE ROBLEDO

Desiree has been at Founders since 2010 and enjoys spending time with friends at Founders House of Hope. She attended Savana High School in Anaheim. In high school, she began reading poetry and journaling. Currently, she listens to music, watches music videos and her favorite musician is Shakira. Desiree enjoys spending time with her mom, grandmother and her children on the weekends. She also likes co-writing her poetry with a couple of her friends at Founders.

TIGERS

Yes it's true that tigers are cute.
But you are stupid if you try to shoot.
It's easier to stay mute.
Tigers are really big animals.
They eat like a pig.
They're too big.
They can't hang on a twig.
So don't bother them
or they will put up a fight
So you better get out of sight.

BREATH

Take a breath and relax.
Don't take the wrong path.
Are we in love or should I take another breath?
Or is it love and are you not coming back?
So I'll take another breath and slowly take my feelings inside.
How many breaths do I have to take?
Waiting to be with you.
One more time I want to once again
take a breath and be with you.
Once more I should have known that you don't love me and
you're not ever coming back.
I love you.

IT'S NOT IMPORTANT

It's not important if you are faster than someone else
or you make money than anyone else.
But love's the most important thing in life.
So if you think you are perfect
think again.
It must be very lonely and it must not be a very happy life
to be your only friend.
So it's not important to be hateful
and only love yourself.
What's important in this world is to be loved.
It's not important to not be important.

RAINBOW

We are all beautiful people.
Each of us have hearts like a rainbow.
Our own path of love.
Rainbows make us happy.
Some of us are looking for the pot of gold
at the end of the rainbow.
We are looking for a peaceful feeling.
Rainbows are special colors that make us feel good.
Rainbows are made of love.

MY HEART

Pain can be very hard for one person to handle.
Sometimes it's worse than to die slowly.
When your heart is traumatized from all the pain
and suffering,
and your cries have not stopped hurting your heart,
and your life is falling apart—
With fear never to live again
and never to love again,
and never wishing my heart was mine.
I will always be broken hearted.

LOVE

L ove is precious.
Love is beautiful.
I wish love would be forever.
Hate seems to think it's so clever.
Always trying to be better.
Be aware of temptation
because it will create complications.
Peace will overcome.
If we all come together as one.

FRAGRANCE OF LOVE

You are the sun in my heart.
    People try to tear us apart.
If the flower can talk it would say I love you.
If I tell you how much you mean to me,
I wouldn't know where to start.
You are a rose with perfume that fills the world
with a beautiful aroma.
So, happiness will take over with love that's off the chart.

JAY DERIFIELD

Jay was born in Los Angeles, CA and attended Montebello High School. After high school he worked part time jobs including Carl's Junior in San Diego for about a year. Jay enjoyed San Diego and then he enrolled in East Los Angeles College and lived with his mother for four years. Jay developed an interest in art while in middle school and his hobbies include reading, art and music. He enjoys an active lifestyle and spending time in the community.

MY SPIRITS

Y ou get me feeling high.
    Like a dove flying in the sky.
Looking out the dove's eye.
Looking for you as a tear drops from the eye.
Like a raindrop falling from the sky.
Your love brings me joy in the teardrop sky.
Your love quenches the life and surrounds me.

BOONKIAT RINUMPAI

OPTIMISM

Optimism is my hope.
And that everybody will one day be able
to get rid of hate.
Positive beliefs about the future and love.
It is confusing why everyone who knows happiness
cannot make it happen.
No one surrenders to their dreams,
and hope they will make it.

ERIC WILLIAMS

Eric was born in Sacramento, CA and was raised by an adoptive family. They moved to Orange County when he was a year old and Eric attended Bolsa Grande High School in Westminster. After high school he was homeless for a couple of years in Orange County and worked and lived with his girlfriend. He worked as a cashier and ended up moving into board and care homes in Garden Grove. Eric has been at Founders for a year and a half. He enjoys boogey boarding, writing poetry and drawing. Eric has a strong love for animals.

AT FIRST I AM SUCCESSFUL

I am capable of my duties.
But voices appear out of nowhere.
And they belittle my thoughts and comprehension.
My job is a cashier.
Although I can memorize the codes and learn the register,
I hear mean, sad voices coming from many places.
Sometimes I laugh.
Sometimes I am sad.
I try to concentrate on my job.
But once again,
it is too much.
Out of work and desperate,
I am glad that although I couldn't succeed,
there is still a place for me to breath.

THE FADE

As time fades,
our bodies grow.
Trees produce shade.
Some people are on the move.
Some people are in the groove.
Not all songs sound the same.
Not all sins are needed to blame.

WITHOUT A HOME

Images twist, combine and fade.
The next day they will be my shade.
But for tonight the streets I roam.
All alone without a home.

THANKFUL

I am thankful for many things in life.
My health is good and I can enjoy feeling well.
My God has granted me friendship.
A place I like.
A peaceful environment.
My enemies are few.
From my view things are looking great.
I've got a clean slate.
My bed is warm and comfortable.
There is plenty of food at the dinner table.
My blessings are counted for.
I'm optimistic when leaving the front door.
Out in the world there are plenty of people.
I hope they have good times without being deceitful.

BLACKIE

Doggy friend you know I miss you.
I hope you're among friends.
I think your life was rough just like mine.
But I know sometimes it was fine.
I still remember your girlfriend Stinky,
and hope you're with her in doggy heaven.
Doggy friend you know I still miss you,
and hope for the best for you.

YOUNG

When I was young I didn't care.
I threw all my problems in the air.
I broke the rules and did neglect.
I stuck out my neck for others who were the same.
Although I did not have my boundaries,
the demons still gathered around me.
If I had the chance to do it all again,
I really don't know what I would change.
When all is said and done,
I can still say at least I had fun when I was young.

THE GIFT

The gift is near.
The gift is dear.
A friend in need.
Is a friend indeed.
So lend a hand.
And do receive.
For all your wants,
and all your needs.

SUFFERING SOUL

Everybody suffers.
You can see it in their eyes.
It's the truth, no myth.
I ain't telling you no lies.
Pain and sorrow hides deep inside.
So that glory and joy can be felt on the outside.
So do not let slide and overflow the pain that you know.
You could hurt a body and stop them on the go.

MARC SPOTO
AND DESIREE ROBLEDO

SHOES

Everybody has them.
They take them for granted.
But somehow without them like a tree we'd be plants.
You can with your friend buy a similar pair.
You'll be just like twins and let the buyer beware.
Some call them dogs.
Some call them kicks.
Some just for guys, some just for chicks.
They're made of nylon, rubber or leather.
You can wear them outside in all types of weather.
Whether for leisure, for sport or for dress you can
always wear shoes to avoid a big mess.

FOUNDERS

Founders House is the place for me.
Schizoaffective is lots of fun you see.
Good food and people,
a great combination.
God's always watching for little temptations.
I love it here.
I hope it won't change,
cause my favorite song is Home on the Range.
If you got time there's something
to do, like picnics on the beach and trips to the zoo.
At Founders House there's a lot of good people,
but you better watch out cause some are deceitful.
You can work in the store for a tidy reward.
You can go to the Docs group,
and even bring your skateboard.
Founders is the best,
I want to live here forever.
It's not a gamble,
no need for a lever.

CECILE MERMELSTEIN

Cecile began writing as a child. She loved reading and took an interest in poetry later. As a child, she wrote stories on pads of paper and drew images to reflect her writing. Her goal was to become a famous author. In high school she enjoyed creative writing at Stevenson High School in Livonia, Michigan. Cecile attended a poetry reading group at Cobb's Corner Bar where she read her poetry on stage and became more passionate about writing. At age 18, she was diagnosed with Schizophrenia and took a Greyhound from Detroit to Lake View Terrace, CA She is currently at Founders House of Hope and still enjoys writing poetry, art and writing in her journal. Cecile's parents are deceased and she regularly communicates with her only sister living in Savanah, Georgia.

MY NEIGHBORHOOD

It is an open universe
where planets place.
In voids made terse
and life is there on every one.
Warping around and orange sun
Is earth, our home world.
Where life teams huge and what's in a centrifuge.
Of stars that shine where we've outgrown our usual old forest home.
Comets fly past distant moons.
And solar systems play their tunes.
And animals who fly can see the sky has a consistency
and no one dare works without still.
Magnificent and enthralled.
Believing everything you see was made serendipity.
Keep the pace, do not allow one to doubt, to make you wonder
how or why. Only forever to know.
Only terrestrials we might outgrow.
This little world and find even more.
What stars forever have in store.

A HEART NOT SPOKEN

I am the owner of a heart in solitude.
I kept it hidden within.
I kept it mute.
I never had time for a sweet, sultry kiss.
I never could rhyme (my soul an abyss)
I cared not for passion. I cared not for pain.
Within me reason. But never a rain.
I could not cry when I felt loss. When angry or hurt, or evil.
Not to be cross.
My heart ejected what I thought was sin.
And all my soul kept so deep within.
Many sugar coated lore from dreams that I had before.
And hatred made me laugh out loud, even when I was in a superfluous crowd.
Before me—men would bow and pray.
And all I cared for was my own night and day.
I lived with Kings and Royalty too.
And love of things was all I knew.
My heart could not fly nor love, nor care.
Even though my soul lived there.
And all my status, and all I owned seemed not to matter.
I lived alone.
And in the mirror I did not see that I had felt the end of me.

REFLECTING ON PAST CHRISTMAS'S

The night is dark, the rain falls hard.
Christ came to give us
the Spoken Word.
And as the stars glow in the sky,
eternity means your soul won't die.

Your soul won't die. Your soul won't die.
God above told not one lie that everlasting life renews
because of the sacrifice of The King of the Jews.

There is a dimension, there is a place
that houses your soul and gives mankind grace.
A special land for you and me made up of God's infinity.

Your soul won't die. Your soul won't die.
God promised. He told not one lie
and knew us as one family symbolized in one Christmas tree.

Look above then. Deep in the sky
at night time to realize those stars on high.

The soul can't die. The soul can't die.

Christ came to save us. Each single one.
His sacred heart of God's own son.
The gift was free if you accept and therefore
paid each little debt.
The soul can't die. You keep your life.

No greater gift. The Church of Christ's life with
everlasting brotherhood.
The soul can't die. We are all made good.
So awaken angels. Shine like stars.
Shine planets.
Neptune, Venus, Mars.
The Kingdom Come!
The infinite sky.
And the soul can't die.
The soul can't die.

OF THE MUSE

The inner mind of every man did not create
the Cosmos Plan.
It won't attest to stars above.
Call itself God or Perfect Love.

It will not shine like unknown stars.
Make consequences out of wars.

It will not spin like long, dead moons.
Make hurricanes or make typhoons.
The mind cannot know the unknown.
God cannot call you if alone.

There is no nature to contrive.
Explain evolving souls alive.

Dive deep in oceans or the sky.
Make permanent in death to die.
Or respect the forest, flowers.
Count the cessation of the hours.

Climb on mountains, count the grains
Of sand upon the dessert plains.

The mind cannot control our times
Or subterfuge the sun that shines.
Or comprehend the last frontier.
All things the mind can prospect fear.
And am of us.
Are born alone.
The soul our everlasting home.

REMEMBERING MY MOTHER

My mother loved me as all mothers do.
Even though her words were few.

She'd bundle me up when it snowed outside
and strapped me in when we went for a ride.

She'd make me hot chocolate when days were cold.
Wrap her arms around me though her arms were old.
Cuddle me if I had a nightmare and joke on Halloween
so I wouldn't feel scared.

She'd bake me a cake for my birthday and taught
me in Church how to pray.

She'd never have any prejudice,
and put me to sleep with a gentle kiss.

You taught me Mother to be proud.
I'm free and I'll always remember that you loved me.

FOR FATE AND MUSES

My captured heart would hurt inside
and in a blackguard I would die.
I didn't know if it was love or an illusion.
Purple—mauve.
Where elves and fairies really swirled
the colors of a forest world.
I noticed unicorns were there, glowing gold
with silver hair.
And dwarfs and hobbits, wizards too.
All my world is all I knew.
The flying dragon when I breathe. Fire.
And they were honest, though called liar.
And angels were the myths of man.
Yet all these things I kept within my secret
like a mystery.
Poor captured heart now set me free.
And deep within, the forest home, all my life,
I've lived alone.
For paradise today is gone.
And human beings came along.
So all the mosaic made a change.
The colors completely rearranged.
And I'm a relic of the past.
A sorcerres, but no spells cast,
can ever again bring these things back.
We are ethynie, the rose turned black.

And birds are really cherubim.
The old archangels caused the sin.
Destroying every living things.
Any my poor heart,
fly on the wing.

Can contemplate what caused it all.
Grace ended and there was the fall.
My heart was good!
But God killed me.
The beginning and end of Eternity.

WHAT ANGELS THINK LIKE

Did you find me?
Hello soul.
What today will be my role?
Will I be a woman grown,
or will I be a soul alone?
Did you catch it?
I have no wants, no desires,
no ancestral haunts.
I don't know where my soul began.
The obvious is,
we are man.
But is that really the only thing?
I am a smear,
High on the wing.
My connotations kept together,
any way or any weather.
Any answer for is me,
just don't give a cruel case be.
An angel.
Yes you, find it's free.
To symbolize a soul like me.

FOR LIBBY
ON HER BIRTHDAY

I love a sister. Sweet is true.
The sweetest sister you ever knew.
In make believe we used to play.
When in the early years of day.
We swam together,
played through the times.
We had our fights so siblings say crimes.
She'd do my hair and I'd do hers.
Sometimes it just made it worse.
We'd play dolls and I liked playing cars.
In the bath tub we'd play Godzilla wars.
I'd watch science fiction on t.v.
My sister liked rock n' roll.
Radio free.
Never does she forget to say "I love you" for my own birthday.
And everything we always spared,
my sister and I always shared.
And kept together, through thick and thin.
Everywhere together we've been.
Even fishing, even summer's long.
She's been my best friend all along.
An no one has a sister like me.
Cute and sweet and happily.

LIFE

Life in the city.
Oh what a pity.
Sobbing my tears away.
And again, what a mess.
If I could just guess the answers to heal every day.
To be on the street where lead pulls my feet.
I watch the police drive away.
My mind is an ache.
To make no mistake.

I'm watching the pigeons today.
Do you love the slums?
Watching the bums?
Tears come easy to me.
What do I do?
Kept by a few.
At least my heart can be free.

GRATEFUL

I'm grateful for my heart and soul.
For friendship and for friendship's role.
I'm thankful that there's peace within,
less anger, sin.
I'm thankful for the world.
I'm thankful for the music.
I'm thankful I have soul and life.
And that I'm free from every strife.

LIVING WITH
A MENTAL ILLNESS

With mental illness,
the pain inside makes frustration, takes my pride,
causes me to cry and scream.
I can't wake up,
I'm in a dream.
The agony of all the pain.
Questioning what could be sane.
The medication is my crutch.
Not sure if it's too much.
The dreams chase my thoughts away.
All I can do is just pray.

BRENDA KISZONAK

Brenda was born in Morgan County, Ohio and lived there until the age of 12. Her family moved to Anaheim CA where she attended Anaheim High School. Brenda enjoyed English Literature and Journalism courses and was editor of the school paper called Anaheim, Orange County News. She attended Abilene Christian University for two years and earned her degree in Communication and Broadcasting. After graduating she interned at KTXS-TV as a sports camera person for a year. She then relocated to Fullerton CA and got a job at Government Channel 3, City of Fullerton where she was a live camera operator for the city council. She was employed there for a year while living independently at the time. Brenda is currently at Founders and enjoys working with Gary Gabriel, CEO of V-Matrix. Brenda began creative writing while in high school and enjoys writing today.

NATURE

On a bright, sunny day,
the sun is so bright.
At night time,
the wind cools me.
The trees sway.
What a beautiful night.

MY LIFE

Yes, once criminal,
dangerous minds.
I was wrong, I was right.
Now I'm in it for the fight.
Been used, abused and scorned.
Been down that road.
Around the world.
Got my life back.
Dreaming of a good life.
I am made for love.
Love is free.
Don't disrespect me.
Wouldn't you know it.
I got it right.

BARRON ODOM

Barron enjoyed playing football beginning at age 10 and attended Washington High School in Los Angeles. He discovered his writing talents a few years ago while an inpatient at Brotman Hospital. Barron's poetry is loved by people and he is inspired by the popularity of his writing. Barron is a new resident at Founders and he appreciates the support and opportunity to write. One day, Barron would like to self-publish a book of his poetry. Barron's mother resides in Los Angeles and his sister is also in Los Angeles. Barron's goals include living independently and working in the community. Ideally, Barron would like to be married and raising a family.

ACHIEVE

You won't get anything done if you just sit around
and twiddle your thumb.
You have to feel good about yourself and feel as if you're the one.
There are many things you can do to accomplish the best.
One thing to remember is to take on challenges and conquer every test.
Get out and win each game with a winning spirit.
No one can stop you at any feat you set out to achieve.

THE BEST OF FRIENDS

I was so happy to meet you at last.
Someone I can hang with.
Someone I have things in common with.
To spend time with or just chill and sit.
We did everything together.
Especially run and play.
Looked for girls together and
just really made the best out or every day.
Can't keep up with the things we did together.
The happiness never ends.
Since the days of youth until now
we are still the best of friends.

KICKIN IT

We can watch some tv together and sit close at night.
Kickin it.
We can compromise with each other and avoid a fight.
Kickin it.
We can dance to tunes we pick out of our collection.
Kickin it.
We can treat each other right.
Sharing love and affection.
Kickin it.
So come be by my side soon and I'll provide you with love that won't quit.
You'll find me with an open heart waiting for you.
I want to be with you everyday.
Kickin it.
I want to whisper to you how love could be.
Kickin it.
I want to serve you a cold beverage that quenches your thirst.
Kickin it.
I want to see you happy,
Through the good times and the worst.

Kickin it.
Kickin It.
Kickin It.

MY STAR

It has been a long time since I shared with you how I feel.
Yes, you are in my heart with a love that is so for real.
Don't you ever leave me.
If you did it would leave a scar.
For I love the way you shine and for always you will be my star.

CHILL

There is no need to come out
as someone who is very tough.
You have to remember that you're not the only one who has it rough.
It will get done so don't be so set on making demands.
Work together.
There's more of a chance that we can make a stand.
Things may get in our way and we admittedly toss out a rebuke.
We have to know we can make it this time.
Tell them this ain't a fluke.
This could take some time.
So be ready to tell them just how you feel.
Until that time arrives,
plant yourself on your favorite seat and chill.

YOU, DAD

I admire the way you worked hard and do all you can to keep us all a family.
It makes me look up to you and proud to have you on top of our family tree.
I look forward to seeing your face.
It just seems to fill me with strength.
But I have to tell you that when you go away
I feel that I have the weight of the world on my
shoulders with no defense.
I thank you for all you taught me and I will
keep you close to my heart.
I love you now just the way I did from the start.
Knowing what kind of man you are
helps me measure out the good from the bad.
And having no problem of telling anyone
that I love you dad.

THE LOVE I HAVE FOR YOU

Spending time with you is all I want to do.
Nothing is too good for us two.
I will never give up the ability
I have to hold you in my arms.
And I guarantee to you
I will keep you away from harm.
I am going to prove to you
the love I have is true.
So expect greatness because
it's real the love I have for you.

NOT YET

I never felt like I had the answers
to all the mess that was falling on my head.
No suicide because I never could imagine what it would be like to be dead.
Walking in the streets under any condition.
Stopped many times to gather and figure out my new mission.
It was easy imagining what it would be like to lay in a warm, clean room.
At that time I had a thought come from God
telling me it will be better soon.
So don't give up no matter how hard the test gets.
Just know that God is not done with you yet.

IT'S OKAY

The time of hardships
add up to be a long, long time.
Many years have passed and you never possessed
enough to share with anyone a thin dime.
What is keeping you going?
A little prayer and a whole lot of faith.
I see you going on now because you
understand that time don't wait.
It's going to get better now.
Say thank you for every day.
I believe now it's your turn to say
It is Okay.

TELL THEM

Tell them you need them
to be on your side
when it's time for you to go.
Tell them you need them to pick you up
when you are feeling low.
Tell them you need them to make your party a success.
Tell them you need them
because you feel they are the best.
Tell them you need them to lift your spirits when you are down.
Tell them you need them because no one else
can fill that space when you are in the mood for some sounds.
Tell them you need them to knock
all the negative feelings away that may come around.
Tell them you need them to help you celebrate
your achievements when you are victory bound.
You can tell them that you need to be with me
because there will be no coming back this time,
and that the love you give this time is so humungous
that it will be a crime.
Tell them.

JOY

Somehow I need to show you,
what you do to this boy.
You give me happiness as if I just got a new toy.
You bring a smile to my face,
one that no one can destroy.
Being with you is all I want,
no where else can I find that joy.

NEVER TO BE DENIED

Someway I fill the need to show you
how I feel about you inside.
That's when you come to be with me
and I am there with my arms open wide.
I feel the need to have something for you when you
come to be by my side.
A loving relationship between both of us where we're opened
to each other, and we don't have noting to hide.
Your love is special to me,
like a groom's new bride.
That's when I let you know there is some love here for you
That you will never be denied.

BY YOUR SIDE

You might think that you are quite a ways from the ones you love.
And so you reach out for something from up above.
People you run into tell you that if
you call upon God you will be fine.
So you try hard to keep the negative from your mind.
I just want to tell you that I am here
and you do not have to rely on foolish pride
I am ready to be with you through
the journey and stick by your side.

PUPPY GOODBYE

When dad brought you home to us you were like a dream come true.
A pit bull dog who did what ever we wanted him to do.
At no time at all you grew to be a great guard dog and pet.
Even though it's been a long time since you've been gone
I haven't gotten over you yet.
It was nice having you running free in our yard, digging dirt holes for bones.
With you gone now it doesn't quite seem like a happy home.
Just like a human being when I think about you I cry.
I learned it was hard saying puppy goodbye.

PAT MCCLOUD

Pat was born in Orange County, CA and attended Sunny Hills High School in Fullerton, CA. He enjoyed art design in high school and college at Long Beach City College and Fullerton Community College majoring in liberal arts, art design and interior design. If you ever call Founders House of Hope, you're likely to talk to Pat because he handles the phone there. Pat enjoys listening to jazz on the WAVE and writing. Pat's family includes a brother in Montana, and aunts and uncles in South Laguna.

Winter's morning.
Indigo.
On yet another gilded morning,
fades away, on this winter's frost.
Locked in my window,
giving way to thoughts of better days with me and you.
This dream on a new horizon,
is about to come true,
On the promise of a sterling rose.
Yet there for the grace of the Priest,
go I.

Tales of midnight dancing on an eastern horizon.
While rainbows and dreams come true.
In early morning's light,
two people on a western shore, hand in hand,
believing in a sterling rose.
When all is not lost,
a sterling promise guides two back to an earlier moment.
Hope gives way to better days.
Mauve paints the horizon on a new morning.
The road to one,
just for me and you.
A Phoenix reborn today.

EARLY MORNING

Mauve clouds.
Strewn across a crimson sky.
Summer comes home.
On another day's early light.
A kiss.
A breath away from knowing you again.
A new day to begin with you.
A thought.
To hold you close again.
In early morning's light.

Dreaming again on a day.
When I dared to share with a dreamer.
Of thee and me on some winters day.
Without knowing.
No one to ask home on these dreams.
Of days gone by.
All hope comes true.
On dreams of better days.
Somebody shared a better way.
A new day of hope, with thee.

In remembrance.
The oven door falls.
A world without fire.
The tyranny of the oppressed.
The third rising of the Lucifer.
A star eclipses the moon,
except for you and me who go on.
To dream of a better day.
A world without hate.

ANDREW KNIGHT

Andy first discovered his artistic and writing talents in high school. He was attracted to poetry like he was attracted to his first girlfriend. He attended Rocky Mountain College in Billings, Montana to pursue art and a new experience. Currently, he has found his passion in writing poetry, abstract art in acrylics and he hopes to compete in his first triathlon soon. Andy's poetry is inspirational and it continues to motivate him and others to achieve their potential. He hopes to extend guidance toward a new generation of young writers to achieve their creative potential. Andy wants to keep motivated by keeping fit and exercising his mind through writing poetry. Andy also draws inspiration from his art which reflects the intersection between music and his perceptions of what it takes to unite the world. The mosaic mixture of colors in his art subscribes to the notion that fabric of colors can be united to create a unified world.

TRIATHLON

Here I go as the buzzer sounds I'm off to the gun blast,
as I tread through the water in unison hoping not to finish last.
My body is an element with which I can swim fast.
It's solely unto me as I try not to get passed.
Stroke over stroke I swim keeping up my pace as I go for the win,
now all I have to do is reach from the bottom and see if I have anything left from within.
As I exit the water and head for my bike I'm in a position that I like,
winding my way along the road I can find myself trekking all alone.
The training that I've done has kept me prepared for this grueling race that once got me scared.
The asphalt burns as my tires plead to tread my stamina beckons in the final meter ahead.
And now I keep my pace as now I am the only one in this race,
meter after meter I find myself in thought what the final destination will have brought.
I grasp onto my goal and see as to what I have brought towards my soul,
for I have crossed the finish line and it is just as sweet this one last time.

DROP A DIME

A bounce skip as my ball moves across the grid,
as I pass them one by one I get closer to advancing my ball to the lid.
The sticky sweat pours from my dome as I get closer towards home.
Pass or shoot now my nerves are unraveling I'm all alone.
I charge to the rim shaking defenders as I go for the rim
going full pace as I make a spin.
I can now say I have what it takes to grab a win
as we've come from behind nobody thought we've had it from within.
I take two steps going up to finish my opponents with a grin
flushing the ball through the hoop I can now say I have two more points for the win.

NUMBER 1 GIRL

From a boy to a girl my love is like a swirl,
capturing her heart making her feel like my number 1 girl.
Her rosy red cheeks to her slim waistline I'm about to make her all mine,
to make her feel fine I could take her out on the town and drop a single line.
From head to toe I'll escort her wherever she may go,
from the top of a mountain to the lowest of lows.
I'm about to put it on this girl like she'll never know,
giving her that deep sensation making her scream out in unison ohhhhh.
Capturing her heart will be like no other feeling my intentions from the start,
my goal now is to keep this girl for the rest of my life through thickness and in strife.
For now we will have no beef unsettled from the start
for she is my number 1 girl.

TO LIVE AND DIE IN L.A.

L.A. L.A. it ain't always what it seems
If you come from out of town you better bring your dreams.
There's many things to do in L.A. from token rides to fishing in the south bay.
This place has beaches where you can surf all day.
You can get around town without a car by bus or train,
and the weather is always cast as sun without rain.
You can find enjoyment by going out on the town,
by checking out a basketball or baseball game in downtown.
There's a party not far away keeping your head bobbying into the next day,
from rave's in the coliseum to club's in Hollywood it's all to the good.
Hollywood can be the scariest or friendliest of places to an out of towner,
depending on his or her approach their name could be placed in lights on a tower.
Growing up in L.A. I've come to see the good and bad side of this grand city.
It has a lot of potential by comparison to other cities of the world.
The next minute you could be by the beach and the next in the mountains.
Its diversity cannot be measured by the thousands.
As spooky as it seems the ways of the world ain't always what it seems,
so if you come to L.A. make sure you bring a dream.
L.A. it ain't always what it seems,
if you come from out of town you'll know what I mean.
Hip hop is all about rhythm and soul,
dropping mad techniques on the mic to back spins on the floor.
There are 4 elements into where one can express itself.

FOUNDERS

F ounders is the place I live where we all participate and give.
Giving and sharing for one another like a band of brothers.
Money draw Tuesday's gives excitement and cheer.
Spending our money wisely saving the rest for the year.
The food comes in many varieties from Chinese to Mexican.
It helps to know a little Spanish when getting in line for seconds again.

In back we smoke taking time to reflect on a joke.
From characters we once knew to the childhoods from which we grew.
From Bipolar to Schizophrenia we are all dealing with a dilemma.
Medications our cure knowing what to take is up to the doctor for sure.

From Irma to Judy we are all put in check when unruly.
And in time we begin not to listen to those who are untruly.

Group time is always played out in a serious way when
Dr. Levy comes each and every day.
Making our troubles disappear he steadily keeps our minds in gear.

Founders is a haven for me now but in the future I hope to move out somehow.
For it won't be long for my illness to be gone keeping my head up right and strong.

MUSIC KEEPS ME HIGH

Music keeps me in the mood from late night sessions to videos on the tube.
The beat keeps my head thumping keeping my body in the groove.
Listening to greats like Stevie Ray Vaughn the feeling I get keeps my body moving on,
to the highest of pitches to the lowest of lows music keeps me in flow.

Whether out in the club or at home music will not leave me alone.
From the base to the snare albums are there to share.
From the greats to Bob Marley to Albert King they chose to follow a dream,
from pouring their souls into the music they bring.

Loving music can mean only one thing to bursting out and sing.
Give me a beat and I'll know what to do from the first ring.
Hip hop to the be-bop has sweet rhymes for the soul.
While guitars help make melodies for rock n' roll.

DJ's control the party whether you're in your car or at the disco bar.
We can all come to appreciate music's global voice which gives us a choice.
Whether we want to hear jazz or funk while hocking mix tapes out the back of your trunk.
Music is an inspiration to all those who want to profile not pose.

MY BABE

My babe makes me feel o.k.
She'll bring me breakfast in bed to go out of her way.
She's the type of girl that makes it fun to play under the sheets,
and I can count on her not to go with another man and cheat.

From her long blonde hair down to the shoes that she wears,
she makes a killing causing all the boys to stare.
My girl is a go getter from working in the morning to going out at night dressed in
leather.
She likes to get it on after we've talked on the phone till the break of dawn.

We make a killing dressed up to go to the show,
and then it's back to the bedroom to play under the sheets some more.
We have a common bond by not taking one too seriously by right or wrong.
Like two peas in a pod she's as loyal as my pet dog,
and she's as devoted to me as the truth in my dream.

Even if we were a long way away we could find the strength to carry on each day,
by writing a postcard and sending it both ways.
We can make it my dear just wait and see,
for it won't be too long for us to get married forever to be.

THE BEACH

As the sun glares down upon the sea shore,
the boys and girls don't know what they have in store.
From beach balls to surf boards this is what summer's for,
to the lifeguards to the beach bunny's there is no other
way to spend your afternoon when it's sunny.

To the girls in their bikinis it makes you hot and steamy,
if I could rub a magic lamp I would have all these girls by one wish of a Genie.
To the pristine water it cools you off even while it gets hotter.

Now in the water I can ride my board without any bother.
Hence the troubles you have when the surf is packed with
men so it's back to the sand again.
Scowering the beach I can now say I have serenity and peace.

As the sun gets hotter people take cover under shade,
this is what I call having it made.
As I look along the water I can see windsurfers and kite boarders,
and the seagulls flying in pecking order.

For it won't be long for the day to be gone,
as the people pack their belongings and head on.

ENGLAND

E ngland, land of mystery in its history.
As the queen rises from her throne she warns the people they are not alone.
From the royal family to the common man we are all a part of this great land.
To the river Thames to Stonehenge the people treat you as a friend.

From Oxford to Cambridge every child dreams of going
to one of these universities as a kid.
Winston Churchill to Margaret Thatcher
we all looked up to them in stature.
The pubs are scattered throughout the country
having somewhere to go when you're hungry.
Soccer and cricket is a home town affair cheering
on your team throughout the year.

The Beatles were a huge success from the grungy streets
of Liverpool to London's Royce Hall.
Having discovered America it was stripped from
our grasp as the Americans defeated us at last.
To knights of the round table to Henry the VIII
we all know when our history took place.
As our neighbors to the North and
West they keep us striving for our best.

The cities throughout England adopt many
cultures from national monuments with sculptures.
With many customs like being Knighted
under oath you can always find a local with a good joke.
While some call England their home tourists are left to roam.
With the cities a bright I am proud to come
from this land making my soul a light.

CITY BY THE SEA

City by the sea Seal Beach
Where the PD patrol and lead
And they don't stigmatize you on your race or creed

There's a breeze in the air but don't let the catch you giving them a glare
From surfboards to Long Beach they patrol with ease
Keeping accustomed the patrons in need
we have all built this city to what it is today

By contributing to its factors each and every day.
Make sure you give respect to the ranking sects
For we have all grown accustomed to the dissident
Fuzz, 5-0 or one time we can all count on you to abolish crime

Public safety is enforced down by the pier
We all sit back and watch the surfers making it clear

Patrolling this city from end to end is an ongoing trend
Thank God we have what it takes to let the healing mend
Keep up the good work because there are criminals out around the bend

LIFE'S CIRCUMSTANCES

As my lifeline expands I am becoming a man.
From my attempts at college I know I have gained great knowledge.
For it won't be long for me to gather strength and have a wife,
and have children in a house where we can build a family.

I am still young and am trying to live a full life and have as much fun.
But my timecard tells me to accomplish
my goals with the strength within me.
Wherever the end comes I know
I have beaten the odds against some.
From now until the end I know from
my pitfalls I will gradually mend.

For my strength of giving I have a lot to share with the living.
We all have a gift and if we share together
we can obtain an adrenaline lift.
Steadily but surely I am coming into my own counting
the days when I'll break bread for a home.
As my hair steadily grays I am still aware and know it's o.k.

As friends come and go I know I have
inner strength to keep the ones I know.
From the dire straits to the accomplishable traits
there are still a lot of risks at bay.
For it won't be long for my soul to live on.
For knowing I have taken on challenges whether right or wrong.

BEAUTY AND THE BEACH

As the water breaks by the seashore
the beat is going on by the police core
From the Navy shipyard to main street blvd
The shipmates have settled down
in this landmark they call surf town

We can all take a grasp on paradise
But the police have an ongoing fight
Its an easy decline from the rough streets of Long Beach
But by going east you can rest on its mile stretch of beach
Called Seal Beach

Taking a bow at the end of your session
The rest of the surfers can take a lesson
To the nitty gritty streets to downtown
There is a beef unsettled on the ground
To the unruly surfers to the punk ass haters
We are all in this to take care of the caretakers

Take a walk in my shoes one policeman says
As you load your gun with lead
Billowing through the streets you can learn the life of the beat
As we have seen any quiet beach town will have dirty wounds
From a mass shooting at a beauty parlor to the robbing of the bank
We have the police to thank
This city will reap the reward as we have the police to thank for.

ESTROGEN

From a boy to a girl my love is like a swirl
capturing her heart making her feel like my number 1 girl
her rosy red cheeks to her slim waistline
I'm about to make her all mine
to make her feel fine I could take her out on the town
and drop a single line

From head to toe I'll escort her wherever she may go
from the top of a mountain to the lowest of lows
I'm about to put it on this girl like she'll never know
giving her that deep sensation
making her scream out in unison ohhhhh

Capturing her heart will be like no other feeling
my intentions from the start
my goal now is to keep this girl for the rest of my life
through thickness and in strife
for now we will have no beef unsettled from the start
for she is my number 1 girl

TO LIVE AND DIE IN L.A.

L .A. L.A. it ain't always what it seems
If you come from out of town you better bring your dreams
There's many things to do in L.A. from token rides to fishing in the south bay
this place has beaches where you can surf all day

You can get around town without a car by bus or train
and the weather is always cast as sun without rain
You can find enjoyment by going out on the town
by checking out a basketball or baseball game in downtown

There's a party not far away keeping your head bobbying into the next day
from rave's in the coliseum to club's in Hollywood it's all to the good
Hollywood can be the scariest or friendliest of places to an out of towner
depending on his or her approach their name could be placed in lights on a tower

Growing up in L.A. I've come to see the good and bad side of this grand city
It has a lot of potential by comparison to other cities of the world
The next minute you could be by the beach and the next in the mountains
It's diversity cannot be measured by the thousands.

As spooky as it seems the ways of the world ain't always what it seems
so if you come to L.A. make sure you bring a dream.
L.A. it ain't always what it seems
if you come from out of town you'll know what I mean

Hip hop is all about rhythm and soul
dropping mad techniques on the mic to back spins on the floor
there are 4 elements into where one can express itself

The shred sled is where I let all my ambitions and emotions run free
I can stand on it all day and everyone will let me be
It's a toy but its' also an instrument unto which I express my life freely

MUSIC

Music keeps me in the mood from late night sessions to videos on the tube
The beat keeps my head thumping keeping my body in the groove
Listening to greats like Stevie Ray Vaughn the feeling I get keeps my body moving on
To the highest of pitches to the lowest of lows music keeps me in flow

Whether out in the club or at home music will not leave me alone
From the base to the snare albums are there to share
From the greats to Bob Marley to Albert King they chose to follow a dream
From pouring their souls into the music they bring

Loving music can mean only one thing to bursting out and sing
Give me a beat and I'll know what to do from the first ring
Hip hop to the be-bop has sweet rhymes for the soul
While guitars help make melodies for rock n' roll

DJ's control the party whether your in your car or at the disco bar
We can all come to appreciate music's global voice which gives us a choice
Whether we want to hear jazz or funk while hocking mix tapes out the back of your trunk
Music is an inspiration to all those who want to profile not pose

WORKING FOR
A POSITIVE FUTURE

Working for a better life to provide for your wife
Slowly you have to realize you need a job instead of becoming a criminal and rob someone else's livelihood

We can all relate when working under pressure becoming a unit reducing our stressors
Whether your a mechanic or a computer programmer working helps build stamina
If we work together we can achieve success by building to progress
Whether a pro athlete or a raiser of a flag on a totem pole working can get you out of a hole

Street walkers have something to live for even if they're called a whore
Broken dreams are scattered throughout the city causing dreamers to want more
The best way to earn a living is to keep your mind on winning
And the way to stay focused is to keep on living

Children have to grow up knowing they have a chance at anything
Giving them the opportunity at life by carrying on and living
With the century starting we have to build a positive future
Giving the under achievers hope that they can become someone of stature

To stand up and fight is a right
We can all live our lives and achieve something out of sight

POPS

From dad-da to dad I know my father is proud of the son he had
   My father has taught me many wise lessons for he is the one I owe great blessings
We have struggled and fought to stay together increasing our relationship for the better
He has given me strength to stand up and fight and gain great knowledge to stay clever

From teaching me to ride a bike by pushing me around the block on his bad knee
I have gained enough speed to ride my bike or anything steadily
Staying focused I can say we have a strong relationship that bond's us
By having a relationship that's unbreakable it cannot be stopped by even a bus

For letting me choose a sport he helped coach me and gave me support
We gained great success by coming in second in the state soccer championship
With my mother passing my father stood by my side in great stride
He helped me cope with the loss by taking over as boss

Knowing that I had to go to college he helped me prepare by giving his knowledge
I didn't give up by showing my father I could accept the challenge with a leg up
Even now in this position I can depend on him
By achieving anything I know I can make it by my father believing in

THE BEATNIKS

The beatnik generation brought a sense of worth for the people on this earth
They became a voice allowing not just the working class but anyone a choice
Either give up and mope or come together and cope
Allen Ginsberg was a poet with a message and his poems
taught people to stand up and be aggressive

Jack Kerouac wrote with a flare giving his generation a positive
role-model in which they could care
Ken Kesey was a visionary expressing himself into his stories

He would also orchestrate one of the most famous
cross country trips where everyone was under the influence of acid trips
As the beatnik's influenced each other they helped people
express themselves whether sister or brother

William Burroughs may have been the best writer influenced
by the marijuana to get higher
As the Merry Pranksters came to New York there was a big celebration of sorts
Ginsberg greeted the Pranksters with praise but Kerouac had nothing to say
While the beatnik generation went on to be glee and gay it was Kerouac who would stray

With Kerouac starting the beatnik generation it would be he
who would fade into transformation
They would carry on and write keeping their followers something to carry on the light
The beatnik generation was one of the most influential times
Beating on the hearts unto which they could say this generation was mine.

GROWING OLD

As you grow older you tend to have more of the
weight of the world on your shoulders
We can all compensate for our actions knowing
there will be a positive or negative reaction

Blending in to the street vibe can make you hide
But knowing you have the wisdom and knowledge
can give you the strength over those that are in college

Being of age is the same as being underage in a way
You can still dance on a trampoline and ride your bike throughout the day
Having a will and a way can keep you striving like the writer Hemingway
He dreamt and fantasized by writing until his dying day

We are all beings of this earth making it worthwhile to find and search
You can always have enough time to accomplish goals for what it's worth
Taking time to reflect is a stigma not to cross paths with enigma
Making it worthwhile to accomplish your dreams either by yourself or in a team

It's go time for you today
So you can become an accomplished being and give light to the unseeing
We are all givers
But when we come together old or young we can
accomplish anything with a simple gesture.

OLD HABITS

B ack in my day I was about no work and all play
I'd be ready at the break of dawn by picking up a
sack knowing that it was tolerance that I lacked

The screws in my head acted dead
But it was really my emotions portraying
my feelings through what I said
The clock was ticking and I knew I had
to make a life changing experience
So I got a job and it helped erase any of my arrogance

I steadily began to like my structured life
And it made the people around me feel
good by doing what was right
I started to venture off into uncharted territories
and my life started to turn into a saga of stories

By working and staying sober I could
now have the confidence to grow older
With my life in full swing I could face
any challenges that my life had to bring
With the comfort level around me I could
now see what opportunities there were for me
By staying humble I could look back
and know I'll never take a stumble

As my 32nd birthday approaches
I know I have the momentum to listen to my coaches
For I have found eternal bliss and
it is my past which I do not miss.

DR. LEVY

Dr. Levy is one of a kind
from his physical attributes to his mind
He can race the ironman faster
than some can drive to Disneyland
He's a cool cat, contributing his time to those in class
and He's never taken a puff of the old grass

He dreams like us you know by having a
house in Belmont Shore with a Porsche 911
And he plans by following his
Jewish faith to end up in heaven
If I can say so myself he has raised
two beautiful daughters with a little help
Nora is his other half as they have stayed together
for thirty years by encouraging each other to laugh

He has traveled the world
and has given hope to the unliving
Because his soul commands nothing else but giving
In other words Dr. Levy is a force to be reckoned with
and there is no other way he chooses to live
From mentoring me as a kid he has given me
an avenue to express myself from unto which I knew I did

He has helped me train for the triathlon
and when the day comes
I'll have the confidence and speed to march on
When I'm old and gray and he has passed
and gone away I'll have the confidence to say
Thank you for entering my life and given me the insight
For you are the one I owe many blessings
and in heaven we can share our lessons.

EMPOWERMENT

By empowering oneself one can start off by using a little help
Demand a little respect for yourself so you can empower yourself
Leadership can be advised by a naysayer causing you not to care
Or you can turn it into advice enlightening your ideas to share

Stand up and be a leader so your followers can be sightseers'
So they can learn from the best giving their finger-pointing a rest
While we lye in shadow our compatriots are fighting the battle
From daily living to a life long of giving we must nurture the quivering

Uphill is the only way to build
For we are in existence to extend our living distance
Breaking barriers along the way we can all become one and not succumb
To a life filled with obstacles growing and maintaining our skills

Passing the torch we can steadily escalate north
Rising to the top we cannot be stopped
For there is no end in sight and we are confident to know it's alright
For this team can swallow the light and march on through the night

GROUP TIME

As we gather in, Dr. Levy's group is about to begin
Cecile and Desiree start to mingle while
Dr. Levy scolds them causing them to cringle
Group begins with Dr. Levy play
fighting with some of the residents
Giving him the upper hand with some
while others could knock him dumb

Everyday we gather round to here the group sounds
Giving insight to one another's life,
it keeps our head up by continuing to strive
By coming to group Monday to Friday
you get to work in our little hideaway
And at the end of the week you can
receive the money you earned
by sharing what you've learned

From Demetrius to Heidi we are all into writing
The Dr. has received enough writing
from us to make an anthology
We will soon have an inscription that will
reflect each and every one of us
A bible that we can all look at in the future
accomplishing a goal that we can all have forever

While we battle on with our personal
issues it's group that we look to
Receiving feedback from the Dr. is easier
to understand than a recipe from Betty & Crocker

Friday's is a day of leisure and a day we can
look back on the lessons from the teacher
Whether you're a resident or patient
you can always learn something
from one another's statements

RASTAFARIANS

The Rastafarian people believe on treating everyone equal
But a battle has arisen between the baldheads and the dreads

The rastas were formed in retaliation from the segregation
They were brought from Africa by the British looked down upon like midgets

In Jamaica during the 17 hundreds there was an uprising
Jamaicans began to retaliate and form a bond to initiate themselves

A struggle to free themselves took place for two hundred years
And finally during the early 19 hundreds' they found a leader

Haile selassie was his name as the rastafarians looked up to him in vain
To this day there is still a common void between the Rastas and the bald heads which
they call toys

Rastas believe in being clean in mind, body and spirit
As they take pride in eating only fish with fruits and vegetables in their dish

Marijuana is used excessively in praise of Haile Selassie
They have also formed a style of music called reggae giving them something to listen
to while they celebrate

As they strive forward the apartheid keeps them from the road side
And back into the arms of one another giving love to each brother

Since the age of nine I cast out to make the Washington Redskins team mine

HIGH PLAINS DRIFTER

When you've got a Stevie Ray Vaughan record you know you have to instantly turn it on
His melodic voice combined with guitar made him a superstar

Heralded as on of the greatest guitar players of all time
He made his guitar wale as if he had just committed a crime

Making his way through the eighties with hits like Pride and Joy and Texas Flood listeners knew he was not a dud
He started playing the guitar at the age of nine not knowing his skills would cause people to emancipate and go blind

He was still a force to be reckoned with even with all the drugs he did
He still managed to keep it under control and carry on with the show

Fame isn't always what he claimed
He just wanted to take after his parent's name

But he found out at an early age that he belonged performing on stage
His idol was Eric Clapton and just before his death he would perform with him

Stevie's recordings and legacy would live on
Influencing musicians present and gone

In my eyes he could not produce anymore
as his name and legend will go down in folklore.

ERNEST HEMINGWAY

E rnest Hemingway wrote vigorously giving us something
etched in our mind permanently.
He served in the military as a correspondent giving officers information
on problems so they could solve.

He was a big fan of the Caribbean by later moving to Cuba
As his writing continued to move ya

One of his pieces Old Man and The Sea became famous globally
He churned out many great novels
but there was something lurking inside him emotionally.

His mind started to churn as the countless shots
of whiskey made his mouth burn.
He fell into a deep depression even though he could still write in session

He had success knocking on his door but he would drink more and more
He knew he needed help but it was too late for him now

At the age of sixty five he would be dead from suicide
by one single gunshot to the head.
As his legacy lives on it was the suicide which was wrong.

His books give a purpose in which they nurture us
He had an undying talent that boosted his bravado to a stallion

We read his books and collect his articles
knowing that he left behind a tarnished legacy is unbearable.

SARAH

Sarah was a girl I was devoted to and respected
But she would turn me down in the end feeling lousy and rejected

It all started in Billings Mt. by being introduced to by a girl named Hannah
You see I was in college and she in high school, getting to know each other was cool

We began to date and irresistibly we would be together without any escape
She would come over after school and use me sexually like a tool

For I wouldn't object for she was good at sex
We would go to the park and play nookie and
would teach me lessons as if I was a rookie

I went to her prom knowing something was up and wrong
How was I suppose to see this girl after leaving Montana
and go to the coast of California

So I came home and said goodbye leaving my lullaby
I would send her cards knowing I would give up anything
to drive up and see her in my car

A couple years later I got a phone call telling me
that she was in town looking for me
She showed up at my door for I did not know what was in store

We would end up staying together hoping forever
But she soon got homesick and left me hitting me like a ton of bricks.

DORA

Dora is one of a kind as she always comes to work on time
She's ready with the sweep of a broom to clean my room

You can always find her listening to the mariachi's
and she represents her Mexican heritage like a G

She always works with a smile and her hair-do is never out of style
She cares about everyone talking to the clients even when her works done

She manages four children while her career is steadily building
As a representative of Mexico she shows her pride well

Dora lights up the room and would steal any bride's groom
Generally she speaks English but she speaks Spanish in dialect

She's a cool chick as her good reputation sticks
We get along good as any of the clientele should

Dora you give me joy as you are the real McCoy
Thank you for giving your energy for
all the clients appreciate you deeply.

HIP-HOP

Hip-Hop can't be stopped
As it is an emcees friend till the end

From the furious five performing live there is something that makes you strive
Beats and rhymes formed from a dialect gives battlers mad respect

Battle rap takes it to a whole other sect
One emcee with more skills can make the other feel reject

Hip-Hop is everywhere whether listening to it in your car or on the juke box at a bar
Hip-Hop heads from the underground listen to rap of a different sound

Radio streams rap but some think it's crap
Others listen to lyricists protesting that you should be fearing this

Hip-Hop is considered an art giving heads something to perfect from the start
We can all give love to the art by never drifting apart

Hip-Hop is broken down into 4 elements
break dance, DJing, graffiti, and emceeing can be practiced by the needy

All different genres of people celebrate Hip-Hop
For it is an art form that will never stop.

DAY'S FULL

Live each day to the fullest
Use your utilities to maximize your abilities and turn it into positive hostility

We can all come to realize what we have inside
We have got to take each day by day and accomplish the journey with pride

Each day can garnish something new
For each one of us has what it takes to perform on cue

When we have found what were looking for, there is still more in store
For each of our journeys there is still a lot of learning to be accounted for

For we cannot succumb to the weak and run
We have got to gather our strengths in store by wanting more

Televised around the world is the trek started from the inner core
But if we drag our feet we will never march north

We are blessed if we perform a good deed each day
But are criticized if we stand in order not moving any way

A gathering is forming upon the horizon
For we as a people must come together and fight to capture the glory.

CITY OF LONG BEACH

Long Beach is a vast city with a ton to see
You could be down by the ocean putting your imagination in motion

Or you could be in downtown soaking in the street vibe with a pipe full of potion
Either way Long Beach has something for every walk of life whether day or night

Stars have come out of the Beach like Cameron Diaz and Carl Weathers coincided for the better
Even Steven Spielberg and Steve Martin would come to Long Beach State to escape

We have the Convention Center, concerts like Audiotistic, and jazz fest
Bringing the diverse cultures of Long Beach into a birds nest

There's ocean front and Cherry Park where all the skaters would meet up to skate
Downtown Ocean properties skyrocket where
your more suitable areas you can make a profit

Shoreline Village and the Aquarium become a children's play pen
As to certain restaurants you want to keep coming back again

There's also an interesting part of Long Beach called Belmont Shore
Where one can walk and window shop never being hassled by the cops

With all the commotion in this city you can always reflect on its positivity
By becoming part of Long Beach you automatically dive into the nitty gritty.

DREAMERS

If your a night dreamer it could be about sex or your next days demeanor
Were all infected with dreams whether there nightmares making you scream

Or they could be positive giving you motivation if you know what I mean
I've had dreams where I'm the center of attention
with a ton of women giving me resuscitation

I've had dreams of me as the devil falling down a shaft from level to level
You can wake up in a pool of sweat where you haven't finished dreaming yet

We can all be challenged in our dreams thinking there for real
When in fact they serve your head information like a meal

Dreaming is an adventure causing you to go deep into your imagination and venture
It's almost as if your brain is playing tricks on you when dreaming you think its' real

However seriously you want to take them, they will reoccur again and again
So be sure not to stray too far from the bedside
for your dreams could be calling you for another ride.

FAMILY

Family support is so important to have sharing your struggles with your mom and dad
You can turn to anyone in time of need getting advice from the one that lead's

Were a team, a unit, someone that takes your feelings and improves it
When were apart we correspond keeping together that bond

Aunts and uncles brothers and sisters the attention
we give each other are adrenaline lifters
We grow together knowing each others personalities
gives us responsibilities to be accounted for

When we grow old there are stories to be told
Giving us enlightenment into how our tempers went from hot to cold

Braving the elements we would go head over heels to provide our family a meal
There is no greater task than to keep your family
from finishing last you must speed up the recovery and regroup fast

Some family bond's are greater than others
But as long as you have that everlasting love
then there is no need for guidance from up above

God can be a source of unity to improve on
But a family must stay in rhythm without any controversy

Giving hope and light can keep each other tight
That's why family is so important giving guidance every day and night.

LEADER OF YOUR OWN DESTINY

We are living in eternal bliss
Where one must maximize their gifts

To reach your goal one must venture to his or her eternal land
So that we can accomplish our gifts wherever we stand

A thought process must take place so that we can gather and maintain our pace
For we are all competing and striving to win the race

A leader can temporarily guide you and give you the strength to maintain your path
But you have to know it is your path and for you not to finish the race last

As you gather your goals it is you that is gathering strength in your soul
We must share our gifts in order to have the power in our lift

We must avoid weakness by gathering our gifts in the pass
Our goals are in sight as we can see the light becoming very bright

Strength is usually in numbers but we can falter in our ways and succumb
Listen to the ways of the world as leaders stood up as one

Bringing a nation under one and it to stardom
We must break the cycle of the old and weak and bring back everyone on their feet.

DREAM AHEAD

S taring through at the hourglass I know I have to make a move fast
To a realm unknown to many I know I can accomplish my goals plenty

We are at a crossroads in time knowing that we have to follow the footsteps of mankind
Lectures and sermons keep repeating what is determined

But we as a people must come forth to commit and direct a course
Where in the world has all the cowboys gone is what Cheryl Crow said in her song

Finding all the do-gooders in this world to motivate
will be a trek giving them a goal and then congratulate
We can generate motivation by lathering and coating
and keeping the ovation standing

Fighting by moving one step at a time we can abolish crime
Then we can gather the leaders and build over time

Develop and pamper the up and comers so we can unite a nation of brothers
Playgrounds, schools, and libraries will give children motivation
to write poetry in their diaries

As each night grows near we know we have nothing to fear
Because we have accomplished our goals by the time darkness appears

It's exciting to know that we have accomplished our goals
As our torch burns bright it is we who know that our goals are accomplish able tonight.

POLICE PRESENCE

Helping those that have fallen from the grasps of reality
As the loyal civilians look on protesting what is wrong

It is the police we turn to when our enduring need is not strong
In a state of turmoil we can stay true to those that are loyal

Making it safe to the ones that are in turmoil
Making their barriers of the Territory their soil

We are a nation of believers, seekers, and achievers
Directing our route is a basis of thinkers

Making a code of the street theirs where they intimidate the haters by scare tactics
We all have a purpose in life but some slip up and die

Whether telling the truth or making up a lie it is up to us to tell the truth this time
Thank you again for keeping us safe from all the violence and crime

For we would not know the way through this state of anarchy which is sublime
Controlling the guns and death you give us that final step

Which is harder to obtain a rep through death and
love of society or one through guns and pain
We are all messengers of God but some give messages
from God to the corrupt and vain.

MY BOYS

Alexander Ave. where I was born amongst the animals
We were cast away making the most out of our days

Derelicts, once we were called Jack, Patrick, Gene, Evan,
Jason and me, 6 of us in all.
Rummaging around the neighborhood we would scour
our territory as if we were up to no good

Our days were filled with sports of all kinds giving us a way to pass the time
The older we got the more confident we became increasing the skills of our game

Women was our target by interaction they made us feel lethargic
We would fight over the most beautiful making the loser feel like a fool

There were no boundaries as far as the eye could see
As we determined our own destiny

Slowly we began to drift and go our separate ways
Some off to college and some working day by day

There's a cloud hanging over us but someday we'll unite in a genuine way
Off into the day we go not forgetting where we left our soul

We were one unit not giving a care if one was Muslim or Jewish
None of us will forget the time we had for it was the coolest.

TREACHEROUS PAST

College bound as I was off to the lost and found
Trekking from class to class through the snowy ground

My roommates and I found a niche chewing that tobacco so hard it made me spit
Beer can after beer can I was losing my degree of an educated plan

By sleeping all day and partying all night we were
the derelicts of the school with no end in sight
Fighting for what we lacked we tried to get back on track

Picking up from last semester, school seemed to be what I wasn't after
Socializing is what we did best going to each and every sporting event

We were hermits analyzing the night doing what we thought was right
Sitting back I knew I had an option either sit back and mope or get rid of the dope

It would be the Navy I would enlist in and begin another trend
I would say farewell to Billings, MT. And swim deep and far for my home on the cabana

Now I was stuck in a whole new world not knowing if I would survive this turmoil
My soul began to deepen as this was a whole new place for my soul to sleep in

I found change to be good as I was on my own two feet for good
As I came to a conclusion it was my life that was not confusing.

TREE TOP EPISODES

Keep your life in motion so you can apply the final coating
Kicking back amongst the treetop my position feels nice and soft

I can see from a distance as my eyes transition into submission
A little creature down below moving awfully slow

It looks as if it's a nut cracker squirrel
I can follow it with my eyes motioning as if it's a girl

Come here little one and bring your family of sons
As I call her coo koo she takes a glance at me in the tree and shrieks as if I'm in her way

Take it easy little nutcracker for it took me hours to get up this oleander
She takes motion moving in the other direction

As she starts to scour the surrounding trees for inspection
The squirrels have seemed to gather below my tree wanting my ejection

As they start to climb I don't know whether to jump
or whether to climb down from limb to limb and take my time
They seemed to of swarm the tree leaving me with only one possibility

As I jump to the ground they turn back around hissing
like they would at an angry crowd
I sprint off into the distance leaving the squirrels
without any beat down assistance.

SCHIZOMANIA

Half of my mission in life is to show those that I'm not crazy but stable and capable
of anything that a person without a mental illness can do
Whatcha gonna do whatcha gonna do when I come for you
I'm a terror inflicting pain but wait it's an imbalance
in my brain so give me reasonable doubt
I know my disease you can go to the library and read about it
Figuring out It's nooks and crannies but don't expect me to be about it
I can explain It's positive and negatives and tell me what you see throughout it

But conjuring up its' effects on my life is like sticking me slow with a butter knife
Praying that one day I'll be cured are the goals I pray for

To the voices and visions that clutch to me in my own separate prison
We are coming all to familiar to what schizophrenia offers by asking ourselves should
we stop him or drop him when the symptoms begin to overwhelm

Bring the gourney quick he's having a fit or should we sit back and let him overcome it
No you imbecile begin resuscitation before he get's all wound up and hurt's a patient

Bringing harm is not what I do but my first victim could be you
So become apart of my equilibrium and don't ostrich size what I have for you son.

Let us nourish and nurture for we have the gift to give like any innocence of a kid
Become a healer before our ill one's begin by plotting to kill someone
As police officers you carry the responsibility to care for people with instability
So go out there and share what you have learned throughout your career.

ETERNAL LOVE

My honey is off the chain no ifs ands or buts
She could be a street walker by the way she strut's

She's the keeper of my soul, say what?
This girl has got style and grace, she'll make you go off pace by one glimpse of her face

By returning her message makes me feel security
like I've got the world under lock and key
Bring around Beyonce or Janet Jackson and theirs no comparison

We get together over breakfast and lunch and it's she
who's in between the sheets serving me brunch
Where are you gonna go babe, the only place is to
follow me to the end of our grave

Music thumpin, body's bumpin she can dance by tearing
the roof off the joint and keep it jumpin
Give her my heart and she'll know how to handle it

Break away my young countess it is my heart you
have stolen and it is you who can keep it until eternal bliss
Stay my love for you are my angel from above

Baby were a match and there ain't no one that can tell us anything but that
Pick up your satchel and hat because where we're going we're never coming back

My heart is what you've stolen
And with our love it'll never be broken.

FACING A DILEMMA

S chizophrenia, how it takes control of your thoughts like your a robot
Making you withstand the pain as if you've just
withstood a battle you've just fought

Schizophrenia, it's a dilemma not something a result of your temper

Schizophrenia, believing your another person when in
fact you're really hiding behind a curtain
Schizophrenia, when you think you've seen the Dali Llama
as the ambulance comes rushing you to trauma

We're lucky we have a place as nice as this so it's less likely for us to start to trip
We count on each other swapping each other's drink to the last sip
We're a team helping each other to believe in a common bond
and to maintain being strong

I'll maintain my peace of mind letting no-one steal it not for even a dime

What's the message of a crazy person, someone acting erratically, emphatically

Light me up that candle and I'll bring my women to her feet
as we dance up out of our seats
f
Breaking the mold of a stereotype is what each and everyone
of us faces on a daily basis

As we face ourselves dealing with challenges day to day
we must complete each and every journey by saying we're o.k.

Sometimes I think we've been put on this earth to gather all that it's worth

Because we have a special gift of dissecting what's true,
we will prevail by sending the real perpetrators to jail

Love of others and of oneself can keep you stable and in good health

We can all become believers of thyself whether your a junkie living on the streets or
a toddler learning how to breath, live as one and not succumb to those that are dumb

HEARTS IN BLOOM

Only the lord can bless me with my first love up above in a way that he does
She was sent to me by an angel posting enough money for me to get out of jail
on bail

From her rough cali's to her natural beauty she is more than just a cutie
From the first time we met, together our plans would be set

For our relationship was deserving of respect
Our love would need no training and certainly no neglect

Take me to my love for it is she that I can't get enough of
If my cards are played right it is love we'll be making tonight

Strike up that match so I can perform foreplay with hot wax
Bringing the night afloat it is us who'll be sailing away into the night on a boat

Keep me close so you can get every drop out of me, the most
A night escapade is what we'll take, making no room for escape

Up up and away as we fly to outer space as two lovers make an escape without a trace
For we have eaten the fruits of Eden and have come to eternal bliss sealed with a kiss

Collapse into my arms and I will show you
The art of making love sent from the heavens above.

MOORE VILLAGE

Moore village is more than just a village
It's an underground Safeway for those in need of a pillage

We roam around Moore house while some have been around longer than Levi's Strauss
But we carry on taking knowledge from the old and turn it into gold

From morning walks to group talks we are all in battle at the pace of the clock
We file in line not to be rude, waiting for the nourishing food

As we have an agenda to be set we all have a deadline to be met
Racing to the clock we all have an illness that needs to be stopped

As my roommate strives to keep his breath during sleep
it is me who watches over him while in need
I was brought here through an act of G d to become his savior as he nods

Friendly faces all around as it makes me feel profound
Daily trips around town gives us somewhere to hang around

As the pretty nurses scour for our medication it is us that is doing our daily evaluation
Life speaks jive but it is each and every one of us keeping us alive

We are going about life the best that we can,
earning a stripe from those compatriarch's creating a life plan

As we narrow around the bend it is G d's message
we must send by nourishing us from what he has cleansed.

FREEDOM

What does it mean to be free, does it mean we can watch any channel on t.v.
Or does it mean we can date any girl freely

My definition of being free is to feel anything emotionally
Even France took the time to construct the Statue Of Liberty

Giving something to remind us for eternity
Trailing in our place were countries that were scrawny

But they wouldn't give up easy trying to take over our economy
We trusted in ourselves bringing on the fight so we could bring on the day of light

Brushing aside the American Indians we could of
fought for hours knowing what we were doing was sin
Breaking the mold they were in a fight to win

As the years went on and the battles were fought there was
no telling which side would be sought as the victor
Soon we would prevail sending the enemies ships back by wind and sail

We were now Americans more powerful than all of the Africans
We stood our ground knowing that our future was out of sight and sound

Bring on the next victim for we are a nation with a strong military system
America the beautiful just sounds groundbreaking.

UNITE

G d bless the US as we step upon the unknown we'll
test the compatriots of our own home.
G d bless the US, make sure we come to a conclusive
end of suffering by giving the body and mind to heal over time.

We have generated a constant thought of consciences
that we will forever reap in the benefit what G d has meant for us.
Loving and leaving a trademark behind thoughts will go on as we manifest in time.

50 states is our focus by living our life unbogus.
Change has generated staples leaving us without shackles
in a level plain with all of our belongings in a satchel.

As we live in suspense we no longer have to peak over our neighbors fence.
But rather share our thoughts with them over a spliff filled with hemp.

Live and love to get respect breathing down the neck of the weaker sect.
Strength and determination will only rule the upper hand
by then passing on guidance to the next man.

Steel a cherry from a bush and not repent what you have done
then you'll end up in eternity as a wuss.

Open your heart and we'll see if you have what it takes from the start.

Cherish every moment because a moment lost is like giving away your beating heart.
Conspiracy and propaganda can make us go blind like maze but they can never change
the determined look on our face.

Violence and maturity will keep the faith by avoiding violence and rape.
Stay concerned because we have to teach everyone what we have learned.

MARC SPOTO

Marc has been at Founders House of Hope for 14 years and he enjoys spending time with his friends at Founders and walking in the community. He attended University of California, San Diego for two and a half years completing his general education requirements. His creative writing began in elementary school where he was a star performer in sixth grade when he acted in a play titled "Tasco in Tijuana." He hitchhiked across the country in search of Ponce Delicatessen in New Jersey about eight months in his 20's. His family relocated to California when he was one year old from Buffalo, NY. He worked in bicycle stores as a mechanic, as a yard boy for a construction company and mowed lawns for a mowing company. His parents currently live in Thousand Oaks and he enjoys spending time with family. His job at Founders is delivering the mail and he loves this job.

GOD

God is great.
God is good.
God can make you act like Robin Hood.

I don't know.
Been down that road.
That's why I'm a horny toad.
Horny toads are great.
Horny toads are grand.

Some horny toads are in a rock n' roll band.

God is sweet.
God is smart.
If you can't get a job,
Try your hand at art.

If your art is no good,
Just keep it to yourself,
Then buy a nick knack for your shelf.

CARS

S ome cars are fast,
some cars are slow.
What's more important,
they get you where you want to go.

Some like a sportster.
Some like a truck.
A VW will do if you're thumbing and down on your luck.

Some cars can exaggerate your sense of style.
Like a red Lamborghini—20 seconds per mile.

When you're in a hurry,
a car can be your friend.
Your mpg will determine what you spend.

Cars are always improving in looks and efficiency.
How much you are pleased
reflects your sufficiency.

EUPHORIA

Euphoria can come from something you eat.
Something you drink or when you dance on your feet.

It can make you pleased as punch or get tossed out on the street.

You can feel pretty smart when you have a holiday turkey breast.

Some say a can of cold beer is what they like best.

Remember to be healthy when you're looking for fun,
like an adrenaline rush from a bike ride, swim or run.

My personal favorite is a hot cup of coffee
cause it perks me up and gets the sleepy mess off of me.

HAPPY GALS AND GUYS

H appy gals and guys.
They open your eyes.
They're not always good,
but it's understood.

To be your friend they try.

Happy gals and guys,
seeing them as a surprise.
They make you smile,
and for a while.

It's like eating cakes and pies.
The more you miss them,
you get so happy you want to kiss them.

They're happy gals and guys.

TREES

There's nothing as good as trees.
Branches swaying in the breeze.
They can be little or tall, big or small.

Maybe have a hive of bees.
Trees might stand alone,
or in a forest zone.

Young or old,
The stories they hold
of things that happen near them.

Even though they don't speak,
each and every week
they never leave
and give air to breathe.

There's nothing as gold as trees.

CHRISTOPHER RICHARDS

C hristopher was born in Harrisburg, Pennsylvania and his family relocated to Beaverton, Oregon at the age of four. While in elementary school, he took art classes at Pacific Northwest College of Art. After graduating from high school he attended the School of Visual Arts in New York for one semester before transferring to the Cleveland Institute of Art for four and a half years where he earned his BFA. After earning his degree he relocated to Singapore for a year working as an illustrator. After a year in Singapore, he returned to Ohio and worked as an illustrator for eight years. Christopher then worked as a freelance graphic designer and illustrator until the last five years. He came to California four years ago from Ohio, living in Santa Cruz for four years before relocating to Southern California.

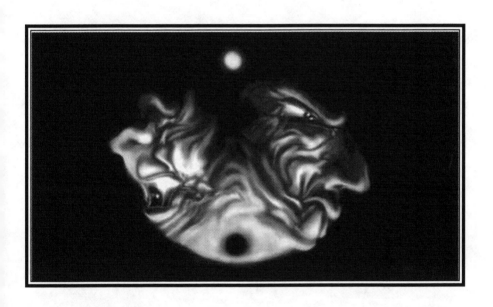

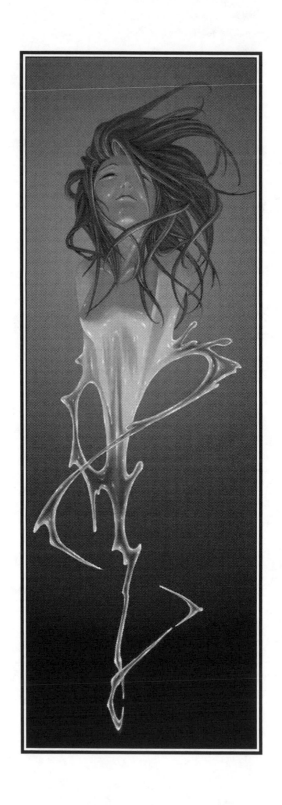

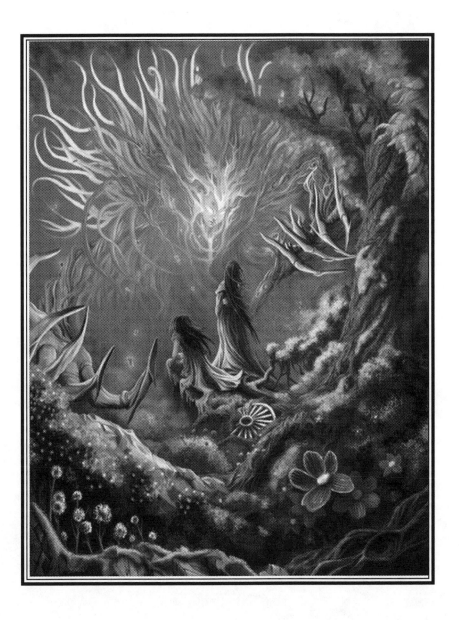

ARLENE GARDIPEE